Good Housekeeping

Light & Healthy

HEARST BOOKS

A Division of Sterling Publishing Co., Inc.

New York

GOOD HOUSEKEEPING
Ellen Levine   Editor in Chief
Susan Westmoreland   Food Director
Susan Deborah Goldsmith   Associate Food Director
Delia Hammock   Nutrition Director
Sharon Franke   Food Appliances Director
Richard Eisenberg   Special Projects Director
Marilu Lopez   Design Director

Book Design by Liz Trovato

Photography Credits
Mark Thomas: Pages 7, 8, 16, 24
Brian Hagiwara: Pages 3, 11, 19, 20, 23, 28
Alan Richardson: Page 12
Zeva Oelbaum: Page 15
Steve Mark Needham: Page 27

2   4   6   8   10   9   7   5   3   1

Published by Hearst Books
A Division of Sterling Publishing Co., Inc.
387 Park Avenue South, New York, NY 10016

The recipes in this book have been excerpted from *Good Housekeeping Light & Healthy Cookbook*.

Good Housekeeping is a trademark owned by Hearst Magazines Property, Inc., in USA,
and Hearst Communications, Inc., in Canada. Hearst Books is a trademark owned by
Hearst Communications, Inc.

The Good Housekeeping Cookbook Seal guarantees that the recipes in this cookbook meet the
strict standards of the Good Housekeeping Institute, a source of reliable information and a consumer advocate since 1900.
Every recipe has been triple-tested for ease, reliability, and great taste.

www.goodhousekeeping.com

Distributed in Canada by Sterling Publishing
c/o Canadian Manda Group,
165 Dufferin Street
Toronto, Ontario, Canada M6K 3H6
Distributed in Australia by Capricorn Link (Australia) Pty. Ltd.
P.O. Box 704, Windsor, NSW 2756 Australia

Manufactured in China

ISBN 1-58816-536-1

Contents

Metric Equivalents

The recipes that appear in this cookbook use the standard United States method for measuring liquid and dry or solid ingredients (teaspoons, tablespoons, and cups). The information on this chart is provided to help cooks outside the U.S. successfully use these recipes. All equivalents are approximate.

METRIC EQUIVALENTS FOR DIFFERENT TYPES OF INGREDIENTS

A standard cup measure of a dry or solid ingredient will vary in weight depending on the type of ingredient. A standard cup of liquid is the same volume for any type of liquid. Use the following chart when converting standard cup measures to grams (weight) or milliliters (volume).

Standard Cup	Fine Powder (e.g. flour)	Grain (e.g. rice)	Granular (e.g. sugar)	Liquid Solids (e.g. butter)	Liquid (e.g. milk)
1	140 g	150 g	190 g	200 g	240 ml
$3/4$	105 g	113 g	143 g	150 g	180 ml
$2/3$	93 g	100 g	125 g	133 g	160 ml
$1/2$	70 g	75 g	95 g	100 g	120 ml
$1/3$	47 g	50 g	63 g	67 g	80 ml
$1/4$	35 g	38 g	48 g	50 g	60 ml
$1/8$	18 g	19 g	24 g	25 g	30 ml

USEFUL EQUIVALENTS FOR LIQUID INGREDIENTS BY VOLUME

$1/4$ tsp =					1 ml
$1/2$ tsp =					2 ml
1 tsp =					5 ml
3 tsp =	1 tbls =		$1/2$ fl oz =	15 ml
	2 tbls =	$1/8$ cup =	1 fl oz =	30 ml
	4 tbls =	$1/4$ cup =	2 fl oz =	60 ml
	$5 1/3$ tbls =	$1/3$ cup =	3 fl oz =	80 ml
	8 tbls =	$1/2$ cup =	4 fl oz =	120 ml
	$10 2/3$ tbls =	$2/3$ cup =	5 fl oz =	160 ml
	12 tbls =	$3/4$ cup =	6 fl oz =	180 ml
	16 tbls =	1 cup =	8 fl oz =	240 ml
	1 pt =	2 cups =	16 fl oz =	480 ml
	1 qt =	4 cups =	32 fl oz =	960 ml
			33 fl oz =	1000 ml = 1l

USEFUL EQUIVALENTS FOR DRY INGREDIENTS BY WEIGHT
(To convert ounces to grams, multiply the number of ounces by 30.)

1 oz =	$1/16$ lb =	30 g
4 oz =	$1/4$ lb =	120 g
8 oz =	$1/2$ lb =	240 g
12 oz =	$3/4$ lb =	360 g
16 oz =	1 lb =	480 g

USEFUL EQUIVALENTS FOR LENGTH
(To convert inches to centimeters, multiply the number of inches by 2.5.)

1 in =		2.5 cm
6 in =	$1/2$ ft =	15 cm
12 in =	1 ft =	30 cm
36 in =	3 ft = 1 yd =	90 cm
40 in =		100 cm = 1 m

USEFUL EQUIVALENTS FOR COOKING/OVEN TEMPERATURES

	Fahrenheit	Celsius	Gas Mark
Freeze Water	32° F	0° C	
Room Temperature	68° F	20° C	
Boil Water	212° F	100° C	
Bake	325° F	160° C	3
	350° F	180° C	4
	375° F	190° C	5
	400° F	200° C	6
	425° F	220° C	7
	450° F	230° C	8
Broil			Grill

The message should be simple: Eat well to stay well. But what is eating well? Every diet expert seems to recommend something different. Most experts agree that it is not healthy to cut out an entire category of foods—such as carbohydrates—but instead recommend limiting the portion size.

Dietary Guidelines for Americans

The U.S. Department of Agriculture (USDA) recommends that everyone aim for fitness, build a healthy base, and choose sensibly. More specifically, the agency recommends that you:

- Aim for a healthy weight and be physically active each day.
- Let the pyramid guide your food choices.
- Choose a variety of grains, especially whole grains, fruits, and vegetables daily.
- Keep food safe for consumption.
- Choose a diet that is low in saturated fat and cholesterol and moderate in total fat.
- Choose your beverages and foods to moderate your intake of sugar.
- Choose and prepare foods with less salt.
- If you drink alcoholic beverages, do so in moderation.

Nutrients: The Big Three

Our bodies need three essential nutrients: carbohydrates, proteins, and fats. Carbohydrates are the body's major source of energy, feeding the brain and nervous system. Complex carbohydrates (including starch and fiber) are long chains of sugar molecules, while simple carbohydrates are single sugar molecules, or two linked sugar molecules. Proteins are needed to help produce new body tissue. Fats store the energy the body needs, but too much of the wrong kind can lead to health problems, including cardiovascular disease. Saturated fats (found in meat, dairy products, coconut and palm oils) and trans fat (found in processed foods via partially hydrogenated oils) should be eaten sparingly, while monounsaturated fats (found in olive, peanut, and canola oils) and polyunsaturated fats (found mainly in safflower, sunflower, corn, soybean, and cotton seed oils and some fish) are healthier and should constitute the majority of the fat in your diet.

Most health professionals suggest balancing your daily food intake with 50 to 60 percent carbohydrates, 25 to 30 percent fat, and 15 to 20 percent protein. The fat quota is contro-versial, however: In truth, the *type* of fat in the diet is more important than the actual amount, but keeping a cap on total fat can make it easier to maintain a healthy weight. Keep in mind that fat is an essential nutrient, so don't cut back too much.

To calculate the amount of fat you can consume each day and still meet a 30 percent limit, divide your ideal body weight (your doctor can provide you with this number) by 2. For example, if your ideal body weight is 120 pounds, limit your total fat intake to 60 grams (120 lbs ÷ 2 = 60).

Penne with Tomato Cream

PREP: 15 MINUTES   COOK: 30 MINUTES   MAKES 6 MAIN-DISH SERVINGS

This restaurant favorite is a cinch to prepare at home. Don't hesitate to add the vodka. You won't taste it: It just melds the flavors.

1	tablespoon olive oil
1	small onion, chopped
1	garlic clove, finely chopped
1/8	to 1/4 teaspoon crushed red pepper
1	can (28 ounces) tomatoes in puree, coarsely chopped
3	tablespoons vodka (optional)
1/2	teaspoon salt
1/2	cup heavy or whipping cream
1	cup frozen peas, thawed
1	package (16 ounces) penne or rotini
1/2	cup loosely packed fresh basil leaves, thinly sliced

- In nonstick 12-inch skillet, heat oil over medium heat. Add onion and cook until tender, about 5 minutes. Add garlic and crushed red pepper; cook until garlic is golden, about 30 seconds longer. Stir in tomatoes with their puree, vodka if using, and salt; heat to boiling over high heat. Reduce heat and simmer until sauce has thickened, 15 to 20 minutes. Stir in cream and peas; heat to boiling.

- Meanwhile, in large saucepot, cook pasta as label directs. Drain. In warm serving bowl, toss pasta with sauce and sprinkle with basil.

Each serving: About 434 calories (23 percent calories from fat), 13g protein, 71g carbohydrate, 11g total fat (5g saturated), 27mg cholesterol, 509mg sodium.

Steak and Pepper Fajitas

Arrange the meat and condiments in pretty dishes and let everyone make his own.

1   beef top round steak, 1 inch thick
    (3/4 pound), well trimmed

1   bottle (8 ounces) medium-hot chunky
    salsa

1   tablespoon light corn-oil spread
    (56% to 60% fat)

1   medium red onion, thinly sliced

1   medium green pepper, thinly sliced

1   medium red pepper, thinly sliced

2   tablespoons chopped fresh cilantro
    leaves

8   (6-inch) low-fat flour tortillas, warmed
    as label directs

1   container (8 ounces) fat-free sour cream

8   ounces fat-free sharp Cheddar cheese,
    shredded

    chile peppers, lime wedges, and cilantro
    sprigs for garnish

• Preheat broiler. Place steak on rack in broiling pan; spread $1/4$ cup salsa on top. Place pan in broiler at closest position to source of heat; broil steak 8 minutes. Turn steak over and spread $1/4$ cup salsa on top; broil 8 minutes longer for medium-rare or until desired doneness.

• Meanwhile, in nonstick 12-inch skillet, melt corn-oil spread over medium-high heat. Add red onion, green pepper, and red pepper; cook until vegetables are tender-crisp. Stir in chopped cilantro. Spoon mixture into serving bowl.

• To serve, place steak on cutting board; holding knife almost parallel to cutting surface, slice steak crosswise into thin slices. Serve sliced steak with pepper mixture, tortillas, sour cream, shredded cheese, and remaining salsa. Garnish with chile peppers, lime wedges, and cilantro.

Each serving: About 450 calories (14 percent calories from fat), 45g protein, 55g carbohydrate, 7g total fat (1g saturated), 51mg cholesterol, 1,060mg sodium.

Spaghetti and Meatballs

A childhood favorite—with kids of all ages. Here, we've baked the meatballs for leaner results. To further cut back on calories, reduce pasta portions.

Spaghetti Sauce

- 1   tablespoon olive oil
- 1   medium carrot, peeled and finely chopped
- 1   small onion, finely chopped
- 1   garlic clove, finely chopped
- 1   can (28 ounces) Italian-style tomatoes in puree
- 1   small bay leaf
- 1/4   teaspoon salt
- 1/8   teaspoon coarsely ground black pepper

Meatballs

- 2   slices firm white bread, diced
- 3   tablespoons water
- 1   pound lean ground beef or lean ground turkey
- 1   large egg white
- 2   tablespoons grated Pecorino Romano or Parmesan cheese
- 1   tablespoon grated onion
- 1   tablespoon finely chopped fresh parsley leaves
- 1   small garlic clove, crushed with garlic press
- 1/2   teaspoon salt
- 1   package (16 ounces) spaghetti, cooked as label directs

• Prepare Spaghetti Sauce: In 3-quart saucepan, heat oil over medium heat. Add carrot and chopped onion and cook, stirring occasionally, until vegetables are very tender and golden, about 15 minutes. Add chopped garlic; cook, stirring, 1 minute.

• Meanwhile, place tomatoes with their puree in bowl. With hands or slotted spoon, crush tomatoes well. Add tomatoes with their puree, bay leaf, salt, and pepper to saucepan; heat to boiling over high heat. Reduce heat to low; cover and simmer 15 minutes. Uncover and simmer, stirring occasionally, 15 minutes longer. Discard bay leaf.

• While sauce is cooking, prepare Meatballs: Preheat oven to 425°F. Line 13" by 9" metal baking pan with foil; spray foil with nonstick cooking spray.

• In medium bowl, combine diced bread and water. With hand, mix until bread is

evenly moistened. Add ground meat, egg white, Romano, grated onion, parsley, crushed garlic, and salt. With hand, mix until well combined.

- Shape meat mixture into twelve 2-inch meatballs. (For easier shaping, use slightly wet hands.) Place meatballs in pan and bake until cooked through and lightly browned, 15 to 20 minutes. Add meatballs to sauce.

- Place pasta in a large warm serving bowl; spoon meatballs and sauce over pasta.

Each serving: About 430 calories (17 percent calories from fat), 28g protein, 63g carbohydrate, 8g total fat (2g saturated), 144mg cholesterol, 520mg sodium.

Glazed Pork with Pear Chutney

PREP: 10 MINUTES   BROIL: 20 MINUTES   MAKES 6 MAIN-DISH SERVINGS

Pork Tenderloins

1/4	cup packed brown sugar
1	tablespoon cider vinegar
1	teaspoon Dijon mustard
2	pork tenderloins (12 ounces each), trimmed
1/4	teaspoon salt
1/4	teaspoon coarsely ground black pepper

Pear Chutney

1	can (28 ounces) pear halves in heavy syrup
1/3	cup pickled sweet red peppers, drained and chopped
1/4	cup dark seedless raisins
2	teaspoons cider vinegar
1	teaspoon brown sugar
1/4	teaspoon ground ginger
1/4	teaspoon salt
1/8	teaspoon coarsely ground black pepper
1	green onion, chopped

• Prepare Pork Tenderloins: Preheat broiler. In small bowl, mix brown sugar, vinegar, and mustard; set aside. Rub tenderloins with salt and black pepper; place on rack in broiling pan. Place pan in broiler 5 to 7 inches from heat source. Broil tenderloins 8 minutes. Brush with some brown-sugar glaze and broil 2 minutes longer. Turn tenderloins and broil 8 minutes. Brush with remaining brown-sugar glaze and broil until tenderloins are still slightly pink in center, about 2 minutes longer (internal temperature of meat should be 160°F on meat thermometer).

• Meanwhile, prepare Pear Chutney: Drain all but 1/2 cup syrup from canned pears and reserve; cut pears into 1/2-inch chunks. In 2-quart saucepan, heat red peppers, raisins, vinegar, brown sugar, ginger, salt, black pepper, and reserved pear syrup to boiling over high heat. Reduce heat to medium and cook 5 minutes. Reduce heat to low; stir in pears and green onion and cook, covered, 5 minutes longer. Makes about 21/2 cups chutney.

• Place tenderloins on cutting board. Holding knife at an angle, thinly slice tenderloins. Spoon warm chutney over pork slices to serve.

Each serving: About 350 calories (26 percent calories from fat), 28g protein, 39g carbohydrate, 10g total fat (3g saturated), 70mg cholesterol, 410mg sodium.

Baked "Fried" Chicken

PREP: 15 MINUTES   BAKE: 35 MINUTES   MAKES 4 MAIN-DISH SERVINGS

For this healthier version of fried chicken, skinless chicken pieces are dipped in a spicy bread-crumb coating and baked until crispy and golden brown. You won't miss the calories.

	olive oil nonstick cooking spray
1/2	cup plain dried bread crumbs
1/4	cup freshly grated Parmesan cheese
2	tablespoons cornmeal
1/2	teaspoon ground red pepper (cayenne)
1	large egg white
1/2	teaspoon salt
1	chicken (3 1/2 pounds), cut into 8 pieces and skin removed from all but wings

• Preheat oven to 425°F. Grease 15 1/2" by 10 1/2" jelly-roll pan with cooking spray.

• On waxed paper, combine bread crumbs, Parmesan, cornmeal, and ground red pepper. In pie plate, beat egg white and salt.

• Dip each piece of chicken in egg-white mixture, then coat with crumb mixture, firmly pressing so mixture adheres. Arrange chicken in prepared pan; lightly coat chicken with cooking spray.

• Bake chicken until coating is crisp and golden brown and juices run clear when thickest part of chicken is pierced with tip of knife, about 35 minutes.

Each serving: About 329 calories (25 percent calories from fat), 46g protein, 14g carbohydrate, 9g fat (3g saturated), 137mg cholesterol, 660mg sodium.

Tarragon and Grape Chicken

PREP: 15 MINUTES   COOK: ABOUT 20 MINUTES   MAKES 4 MAIN-DISH SERVINGS

Serve with steamed broccoli and orzo or a white and wild rice blend.

4	medium skinless, boneless chicken breast halves (1¼ pounds)
½	teaspoon salt
¼	teaspoon coarsely ground black pepper
1	teaspoon olive oil
2	teaspoons margarine or butter
3	medium shallots, finely chopped (⅓ cup)
¼	cup dry white wine
¼	cup chicken broth
¼	cup half-and-half or light cream
1	cup seedless red and/or green grapes, each cut in half
1	tablespoon chopped fresh tarragon

• Sprinkle chicken with ¼ teaspoon salt and the pepper.

• In nonstick 12-inch skillet, heat oil over medium-high heat until hot. Add chicken and cook 6 minutes. Reduce heat to medium; turn chicken over and cook until chicken is golden brown and loses its pink color throughout, 6 to 8 minutes longer. Transfer chicken to platter and keep warm.

• In same skillet, melt margarine over medium-low heat. Add shallots and remaining ¼ teaspoon salt; cook, stirring, until tender and golden, 3 to 5 minutes. Stir in wine; cook 30 seconds. Stir in broth, half-and-half, grapes, and tarragon. Return chicken to skillet; heat through.

Each serving: About 255 calories (28 percent calories from fat), 34g protein, 10g carbohydrate, 8g total fat (2g saturated), 87mg cholesterol, 455mg sodium.

Grilled Chicken Breasts with Plum Salsa

PREP: 20 MINUTES PLUS MARINATING   GRILL: 10 TO 12 MINUTES   MAKES 4 MAIN-DISH SERVINGS

Here's a quick dish that turns ordinary chicken into the specialty of the house. (The plum salsa can also be used to spice up plain fish and seafood dishes.)

2	tablespoons seasoned rice vinegar
1/2	teaspoon salt
1/8	teaspoon coarsely ground black pepper
4	medium skinless, boneless chicken breast halves (11/4 pounds)
1	pound ripe purple and/or green plums (4 medium), chopped
1/4	cup finely chopped red onion
1/4	cup finely chopped yellow pepper
1/4	cup loosely packed fresh cilantro leaves, finely chopped
1	jalapeño chile, seeded and finely chopped
	mixed baby greens (optional)

• In pie plate, with wire whisk or fork, combine vinegar, salt, and black pepper. Spoon half of vinegar mixture into medium bowl. Add chicken breasts to mixture in pie plate, turning to coat. Cover and refrigerate 30 minutes to marinate, turning occasionally.

• Meanwhile, prepare grill and spray grill rack (away from heat source) with nonstick cooking spray. Prepare the plum salsa: Stir plums, red onion, yellow pepper, cilantro, and jalapeño into vinegar mixture left in bowl. Set plum salsa aside.

• Place chicken breasts on grill over medium heat; discard marinade in pie plate. Grill chicken, turning once, until chicken loses its pink color throughout, 10 to 12 minutes. (If using a grill pan, spray pan with nonstick cooking spray and heat over medium heat until hot but not smoking. Add chicken breasts and cook, turning once, until chicken loses its pink color throughout, 10 to 12 minutes.)

• To serve, place chicken on a bed of mixed baby greens if you like, and spoon plum salsa on top.

Each serving: About 245 calories (15 percent calories from fat), 36g protein, 14g carbohydrate, 4g total fat (1g saturated), 96mg cholesterol, 550mg sodium.

Turkey Meat Loaf

PREP: 20 MINUTES   BAKE: 1 HOUR   MAKES 8 MAIN-DISH SERVINGS

1	tablespoon olive oil
2	medium stalks celery, finely chopped
1	small onion, finely chopped
2	garlic cloves, finely chopped
3/4	teaspoon ground cumin
1 1/2	pounds ground turkey breast
1/3	cup fresh bread crumbs
1/3	cup fat-free (skim) milk
1/3	cup bottled salsa
1	large egg white
1/2	teaspoon salt
1/2	teaspoon coarsely ground black pepper
1/4	cup ketchup
1	teaspoon Dijon mustard

• In nonstick 10-inch skillet, heat oil over medium heat. Add celery and onion; cook, stirring often, until vegetables are tender, 10 minutes. Add garlic and cumin; cook, stirring, 30 seconds. Set vegetable mixture aside to cool slightly.

• Preheat oven to 350°F. In large bowl, with hands, mix vegetable mixture, ground turkey, bread crumbs, milk, salsa, egg white, salt, and pepper until well combined but not overmixed.

• In small bowl, mix ketchup and mustard; set aside.

• In 13" by 9" metal baking pan, shape meat mixture into 9" by 5" loaf. Spread ketchup mixture over top of loaf. Bake meat loaf until meat thermometer inserted in center registers 160°F, about an hour (temperature will rise to 165°F upon standing). Let meat loaf stand 10 minutes before removing from pan and slicing.

Each serving: About 145 calories (25 percent calories from fat), 20g protein, 5g carbohydrate, 4g total fat (1g saturated), 45mg cholesterol, 400mg sodium.

Baked Scrod with Fennel and Potatoes

PREP: 15 MINUTES   BAKE: 55 MINUTES   MAKES 4 MAIN-DISH SERVINGS

A simple dish that only needs a green salad to be a complete meal.

1$1/2$	pounds red potatoes (4 large), thinly sliced
1	medium fennel bulb (1 pound), trimmed and thinly sliced, feathery tops reserved
1	garlic clove, finely chopped
2	tablespoons olive oil
$3/4$	plus $1/8$ teaspoon salt
$1/2$	teaspoon coarsely ground black pepper
4	pieces scrod fillet (5 ounces each)
1	large ripe tomato (8 ounces), seeded and chopped

• Preheat oven to 425°F. In shallow 2$1/2$-quart baking dish, toss potatoes, fennel, garlic, oil, $3/4$ teaspoon salt, and $1/4$ teaspoon pepper until well combined; spread evenly in baking dish. Bake, stirring once, until vegetables are tender and lightly browned, about 45 minutes.

• With tweezers, remove any bones from scrod. Sprinkle scrod with remaining $1/8$ teaspoon salt and remaining $1/4$ teaspoon pepper. Arrange on top of potato mixture. Bake until fish is just opaque throughout, 10 to 15 minutes. Sprinkle with tomato and garnish with reserved fennel tops.

Each serving: About 335 calories (21 percent calories from fat), 30g protein, 35g carbohydrate, 8g total fat (1g saturated), 61mg cholesterol, 679mg sodium.

Quick Seafood Stew

PREP: 10 MINUTES   COOK: 20 MINUTES   MAKES 4 MAIN-DISH SERVINGS

1¼   pounds all-purpose potatoes, peeled and cut into ½-inch pieces

1   can (14½ ounces) chunky tomatoes with olive oil, garlic, and spices

1   can (14½ ounces) chicken broth or 1¾ cups homemade

⅓   cup dry white wine

16   large mussels, scrubbed and debearded

16   large shrimp, shelled and deveined, with tail part of shell left on, if you like

1   piece cod fillet (12 ounces), cut into 2-inch pieces

1   tablespoon chopped fresh parsley leaves

• In 2-quart saucepan, heat potatoes and enough *water* to cover to boiling over high heat. Reduce heat to low; cover and simmer until potatoes are tender, 5 to 8 minutes; drain.

• Meanwhile, in 5-quart Dutch oven, heat tomatoes with their liquid, broth, and wine to boiling over high heat. Add mussels; reduce heat to medium. Cover and simmer until mussels open, 3 to 5 minutes, transferring mussels to bowl as they open. Discard any mussels that do not open.

• Add shrimp and cod to Dutch oven; cover and cook until shrimp and cod are just opaque throughout, 3 to 5 minutes. Add potatoes and mussels; heat through. Sprinkle with parsley.

Each serving: About 305 calories (15 percent calories from fat), 35g protein, 28g carbohydrate, 5g total fat (0g saturated), 136mg cholesterol, 965mg sodium.

Easy Barbecued Beans and Rice

PREP: 15 MINUTES   COOK: 25 MINUTES   MAKES 6 MAIN-DISH SERVINGS

This vegetarian skillet dinner is especially good with a rich, smoky barbecue sauce.

3/4   cup regular long-grain rice

1   tablespoon vegetable oil

1   medium green pepper, cut into 1/2-inch pieces

1   medium red pepper, cut into 1/2-inch pieces

1   medium onion, chopped

1   can (15 to 19 ounces) black beans, rinsed and drained

1   can (15 to 19 ounces) red kidney beans, rinsed and drained

1   can (15 to 19 ounces) garbanzo beans, rinsed and drained

1   can (15 to 16 ounces) pink beans, rinsed and drained

1   can (14 1/2 ounces) no-salt-added stewed tomatoes

1   cup water

1/2   cup bottled barbecue sauce

- In 2-quart saucepan, prepare rice as label directs but do not add butter or margarine.

- Meanwhile, in 12-inch skillet, heat oil over medium heat until hot. Add peppers and onion and cook, stirring, until tender. Add black beans, red kidney beans, garbanzo beans, pink beans, stewed tomatoes, water, and barbecue sauce; heat to boiling over high heat. Reduce heat to low; cover and simmer 15 minutes.

- Spoon rice into center of beans. Before serving, stir to combine rice and bean mixture.

Each serving: About 355 calories (13 percent calories from fat), 16g protein, 61g carbohydrate, 5g total fat (1g saturated), 0mg cholesterol, 790mg sodium.

Vegetarian Tortilla Pie

PREP: 8 MINUTES   BAKE: 12 MINUTES   MAKES 4 MAIN-DISH SERVINGS

This dish can be assembled in a jiffy, thanks to its no-cook filling of canned black beans and corn, prepared salsa, and pre-shredded Monterey Jack cheese.

1   jar (12 ounces) medium salsa

1   can (8 ounces) no-salt-added tomato sauce

1   can (15 to 16 ounces) no-salt-added black beans, rinsed and drained

1   can (15¹/4 ounces) no-salt-added whole-kernel corn, drained

1/2   cup packed fresh cilantro leaves

4   (10-inch) low-fat flour tortillas

6   ounces reduced-fat Monterey Jack cheese, shredded (1¹/2 cups)

     reduced-fat sour cream (optional)

• Preheat oven to 500°F. Spray 15¹/2" by 10¹/2" jelly-roll pan with nonstick cooking spray.

• In small bowl, mix salsa and tomato sauce. In medium bowl, mix black beans, corn, and cilantro.

• Place 1 tortilla in prepared jelly-roll pan. Spread one-third of salsa mixture over tortilla. Top with one-third of bean mixture and one-third of cheese. Repeat layering 2 more times, ending with last tortilla.

• Bake pie until cheese melts and filling is heated through, 10 to 12 minutes. Serve with reduced-fat sour cream if you like.

Each serving without sour cream: About 440 calories (23 percent calories from fat), 25g protein, 65g carbohydrate, 11g total fat (5g saturated), 30mg cholesterol, 820mg sodium.

Tex-Mex Cobb Salad

PREP: 30 MINUTES   MAKES 4 MAIN-DISH SERVINGS

Warm Southwestern accents give this classic a new attitude.

1/4   cup fresh lime juice

2   tablespoons chopped fresh cilantro leaves

4   teaspoons olive oil

1   teaspoon sugar

1/4   teaspoon ground cumin

1/4   teaspoon salt

1/4   teaspoon coarsely ground black pepper

1   medium head romaine lettuce (1 1/4 pounds), trimmed and leaves cut into 1/2-inch-wide strips

1   pint cherry tomatoes, each cut into quarters

12   ounces cooked skinless roast turkey meat, cut into 1/2-inch pieces (2 cups)

1   can (15 to 19 ounces) black beans, rinsed and drained

2   small cucumbers (6 ounces each), peeled, seeded, and sliced 1/2 inch thick

- Prepare dressing: In small bowl, with wire whisk, combine lime juice, cilantro, oil, sugar, cumin, salt, and pepper.

- Place lettuce in large serving bowl. Arrange tomatoes, turkey, black beans, and cucumbers in rows over lettuce. Just before serving, toss salad with dressing.

Each serving: About 310 calories (20 percent calories from fat), 39g protein, 32g carbohydrate, 7g total fat (1g saturated), 71mg cholesterol, 505mg sodium.

Index